SMALL CATS

ANIMAL FAMILIES

SMALL CATS

Markus Kappeler

Gareth Stevens Publishing
MILWAUKEE

A N I M A L F A M I L I E S

For a free color catalog describing Gareth Stevens' list of high-quality books, call 1-800-341-3569 (USA) or 1-800-461-9120 (Canada).

The editor would like to extend special thanks to Elizabeth S. Frank, Curator of Large Mammals at the Milwaukee County Zoo, Milwaukee, Wisconsin, for her kind and professional help with the information in this book.

Library of Congress Cataloging-in-Publication Data

Kappeler, Markus, 1953-
    [Kleinkatzen. English]
    Small cats / Markus Kappeler.
      p. cm. — (Animal families)
    Translation of: Kleinkatzen.
    Includes bibliographical references and index.
    Summary: Describes members of the twenty-nine different species known as "small" cats, including the bobcat, lynx, puma, and ocelot.
    ISBN 0-8368-0843-6
    1. Felidae—Juvenile literature. [1. Felidae. 2. Cats.]
  I. Title. II. Series.
QL737.C23K3713 1992
599.74'428—dc20   92-10655

North American edition first published in 1992 by
Gareth Stevens Publishing
1555 North RiverCenter Drive, Suite 201
Milwaukee, Wisconsin 53212, USA

Series editor: Patricia Lantier-Sampon
Editor: Barbara J. Behm
Translated from the German by Jamie Daniel
Editorial assistants: Diane Laska and Andrea Schneider
Editorial consultant: Elizabeth S. Frank

Printed in the United States of America
1 2 3 4 5 6 7 8 9 98 97 96 95 94 93 92

Picture Credits
Lisbeth Bührer—2, 4, 5; Bruce Coleman—31: Bauer 15 (jungle cat), 18: Cubitt 15 (clouded leopard), 38: Erize 15 (Geoffroy's cat), 34, 35: Foott 33: L.L. Rue III 15 (puma): Williams 15 (African black-footed cat, African golden cat, fishing cat, marbled cat, margay, Pampas cat, rust cat), 24, 25, 27, 28, 30; Delikat-Katzennahrung—14 (Russian blue, Rex Devon, Persian Colorpoint, Abyssinian, Persian Red-shaded Cameo); DRK-Photo—Krasemann 36, 37; EMB Archive—private collection 6-7, 8, 9 (upper and lower); Andreas Fischer-Nagel—11 (upper and lower), 12 (upper); Jacuna—Arthus-Bertrand 15 (wild cat): Mero 14 (Carthusian and Burmese); Visage 15 (lynx); Varin-Visage 15 (jaguarundi and ocelot), 29, 32: Ferrero cover, 15 (leopard cat), 26: Kerneis 21 (lower): Labat 22: Petter 15 (sand cat), 16 (left), 19 (left): Varin 15 (serval), 21 (upper), 23 (left and right): Visage 15 (Pallas' cat), 20; L.W.W. Louwman—16 (right); NHPA—Bannister 19 (right); Hans Reinhard—1, 10-11 (upper and lower), 12 (lower), 13 (upper and lower), 14 (Siamese), 15 (house cat), 17, 40.

Table of Contents

What Is a "Small Cat"?

Thirty-six species of cats live in various places around the world. Twenty-nine of these species are known as "small" cats. The remaining seven species of the cat family include the five "big" cats — the lion, tiger, leopard, jaguar, and snow leopard — and two cats that fit neither category — the clouded leopard and the cheetah.

Scientists disagree about how many types of cats currently inhabit the earth. They also disagree on how all these species of cats are related to each other. This book refers to a relatively simple grouping of the cat family used by many scientists.

The use of the term *small* when referring to the small cats can sometimes be confusing. It is true that most of the smaller cats belong to this family. However, the largest small cat, the puma, is bigger than the smallest big cat, the snow leopard!

Types of Small Cats

The small cat family includes the powerful puma, the tiny black-footed cat, the beautifully spotted ocelot, the plain-colored desert lynx, the long-legged serval, and the long-bodied jaguarundi. Several small cats, such as the South American mountain cat and the red or Borneo cat, have never been captured for study. Therefore, scientists are not sure what they look like. We know of their existence from a few pelts and skeletons and eyewitness details told by native peoples.

More information is available about some of the other small cats. For example, we know quite a bit about the African serval, since servals have been successfully raised in zoos for many years. The same is true for the lynx, and studies have also been made of the lynx in the wild. Precise information has been gathered through the use of small radio transmitters attached to the animals.

The house cat is the small cat most widely studied. People everywhere are familiar with the image of a cat waiting patiently for hours outside a mouse hole. Almost everyone has stroked the fur of a happily purring cat at one time or another.

The house cat is in many ways representative of all small cats. Other small cats behave much like house cats, whether they are sand cats in the desert, Pallas' cats on the plains, or leopard cats in the forest. There are more than thirty breeds of house cats. These breeds are generally classified as either long-haired or short-haired.

All but a few cat breeds belong to the short-haired group. These short-haired cats include tabbies, black cats, and Russian blue or Maltese cats, to name just a few. Two of the cats in the long-haired group are Persian and Angora cats.

The house cat is affectionate but reserved. It is also very intelligent and has an excellent memory. And, in general, a cat is more independent than a dog. It has a strong homing instinct and good grooming habits.

The 3,500-year-old Sphinx of Giza guards the famous Egyptian pyramids. At 65.6 feet (20 m) tall and 241 feet (73.5 m) long, it is the largest cat figure in existence.

Origins of the House Cat

House cats are descended from a North African wild cat called the Nubian dun cat. About four thousand years ago in Egypt, some of these cats befriended people. Stories say these wild cats could not resist the fat mice that ate the Egyptians' stored grain. The ancient Egyptians greatly admired these wild cats and proclaimed them sacred animals. Anyone who killed a cat was severely punished. When a cat died, its owner would cut off all of his or her own hair as a sign of mourning. Animals that died were often buried in valuable wooden coffins. Some were even entombed in elaborate mummy cases. Mummified mice were also buried with these cats to provide food on the journey after death.

In time, the domesticated dun cats spread all along the great trade routes, from the Middle East to China and southern Europe. Two thousand years ago, they had already become beloved house pets to the Romans. Later, the cats made their way across the Alps into central Europe. In central Europe, they successfully interbred with the wild cats that lived there. Many of today's farm cats look more like the European wild cats than the Nubian dun cats of North Africa.

A Minimum of Change

House cats have changed very little since they began living with humans. In fact, it would still be very easy for these domesticated cats to return to the wild and their original ways of life if humans suddenly stopped caring for them. House cats have never become completely dependent upon people. They remain the same self-sufficient, independent, and puzzling animals they have always been.

The house cat has remained independent throughout the centuries partly because of people. That is, humans have never bred the house cat to perform specific tasks. Some species of dogs, on the other hand, have been bred to do certain things, such as help with the hunt. Dogs proved to be useful to humans, so dogs continued to be bred in accordance with human needs.

Cats are different. They help humans by catching mice, but they are cared for by humans mainly for the joy they bring. Cats can be characterized as "luxury" domestic animals as opposed to dogs, the "useful" domestic animals.

Stalking Is Their Profession

The entire family of small cats is made up of predators. Unlike many other animals, cats do not eat leaves, grass, fruit, or other vegetable matter. In the wild, therefore, a small cat's meals consist of fresh meat. But fresh meat doesn't simply fall out of a tree, and it is not possible for a cat to simply sit down and fill its stomach in any one specific place. Its meals have legs and wings and immediately bolt off to safety when a hungry cat comes near. The cat must catch its prey whenever it becomes hungry. The house cat in the wild needs not only good hunting techniques but also hunting equipment. Nature has provided the cat with perfect examples of both.

Hunting Techniques

Unlike dogs, cats are not the type of hunters that follow their prey animals over long distances until they are exhausted. Cats are stalkers that sneak up on their prey silently and catch them in a surprise attack. A cat will move slowly and silently through its territory. It will carefully watch and listen for any noticeable movement or sound. Sometimes it will lie patiently in wait in one spot if it knows that prey animals occasionally pass by. If the cat sees a potential victim, it will approach the animal very, very carefully. It will use every rock, tree, and clump of grass as a cover. It crouches low, lurking and creeping, until it is finally so close that it can capture its prey with a single, fluid pounce. For the victim, the sudden attack often seems to come from nowhere. It has no time to make any attempt to flee or to protect itself. At the very moment the victim realizes what is happening, the cat has already caught it. Sharp claws on the cat's front paws seize the prey. Then the prey is killed with a powerful bite to the spinal cord or the jugular vein. Almost any small animal that crosses the path of the house cat in the wild can become a victim. Prey is usually mice and small birds, since there are usually large numbers

a cat. When the house cat is on the prowl, all small animals in the surrounding area need to be on their guard.

Hunting Equipment

The cat has excellent tools for hunting. First, it has sharp, crescent-shaped claws. These claws are useful tools designed for the cat to firmly grasp its prey. When the cat is relaxed, the claws stay hidden in protective pockets of the cat's skin. This keeps the claws from touching the ground when the cat is walking, which would dull the edges. The claws are quickly extended by special muscles when the cat is ready to pounce on its prey. All cats know the great importance of their claws and use every opportunity to sharpen them.

The cat's eyes provide a second valuable hunting tool. The images a cat sees are six times as sharp as those a human sees. The light sensitivity of a cat's eyes is also six times greater than that of humans. This enables the cat to go hunting at night even though it is pitch dark. A reflective layer of tissue in the cat's eye, called a *tapetum lucidum*, or "carpet of light," plays an important role. This layer reflects any beam of light away from the back of the eye, much like a mirror. This means that the part of the eye called the *retina* is affected twice by every source of light — once when it enters the eye, and again when it bounces back off the reflective layer. The tapetum lucidum is responsible for the way a cat's eyes seem to light up in the darkness when the cat looks into bright light such as a car's headlights.

of both of these in the areas cats inhabit. Cats will also eat grasshoppers and butterflies, lizards and frogs, moles and rats. Even squirrels and young rabbits are not safe from

The cat's sharp, pointed teeth are also valuable tools for hunting. As a natural predator, the cat does not chew its food, but rather tears it apart after capture. Its teeth are specially suited for this purpose and enable the cat to stab and cut its prey.

Another important piece of equipment for the cat is something it doesn't have — a noticeable body odor. Cats pay special attention to their physical hygiene. They repeatedly clean their coats and carefully remove any foreign particles found there. This thorough cleanliness serves a purpose. Many of the cat's prey have an excellent sense of smell. They would be able to smell the stalking cat and hide long before the cat was close enough to pounce. Because the cat has so carefully cleaned itself, the prey it stalks does not smell the cat. The hunt is successful for the cat because the prey is completely surprised by the attack.

The cat is a masterful hunter that seldom suffers from a shortage of food. Because of this, it can spend the greater part of the day — often eighteen hours or more — sound asleep. A cat has plenty of leisure time. It is so good at hunting that it is able to hunt almost as a pastime.

Every Cat for Itself
The house cat is not a herd animal like the cow. Nor is it a pack animal like the dog. The house cat is a loner. Each cat lives and hunts only for itself. There is a good reason for this. As a loner, the cat has a better chance of stalking its prey unnoticed and catching it

suddenly by surprise. This would be more difficult to do in a herd or a pack.

The cat is also very loyal to the area in which it lives. It prefers to spend its entire lifetime in one familiar, fixed area where it can find everything it needs to survive. The cat knows where it will be most likely to find prey, where it will be able to have the best view of the area, where it can hide if there is danger, and where it can take a nap without being disturbed. These conditions make the cat's life much easier than if it has to wander aimlessly through a larger area, never knowing where to look for prey, where to hide while stalking, or where to find shelter.

The cat will not claim all the territory it lives and hunts in for itself alone. It will

Below: If a cat needs its claws, they appear with lightning speed to become a powerful weapon (upper). When it walks, its claws recede and are protected by surrounding pockets of skin (lower).

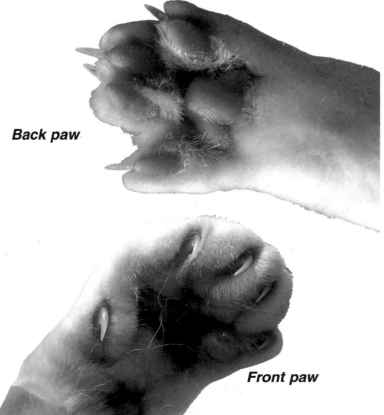

Back paw

Front paw

defend only the areas close to its usual sleeping place and the place it chooses to give birth to its young. It usually will not bother other cats if they merely pass through its hunting territory. A cat will defend the territory, however, if there is continuous conflict with another cat. This can happen if another cat constantly scares away a cat's prey animals.

It is not difficult for cats to stay out of each other's way. Although several cats will usually use the same hiding places and stalking paths, unwanted encounters seldom occur. In such a situation, the cats' high-performance eyes serve them well. Their keen eyesight allows cats to recognize each other even from far away. Scent marks also play an important role. The males in particular repeatedly spray clumps of grass, stones, and other obvious landmarks with

their pungent urine. All other cats living in the area can tell from the scent marking who has passed by and when.

The Mating Ritual

It is only natural for house cats to occasionally give up their solitary lives. This happens whenever the cats feel the urge to mate and care for offspring.

Females that are ready to mate will make it known by howling that they are looking for a companion. The tomcats, or males, respond with their own low-pitched howling, expressing their own urgent need to find a mate. Heated fights often break out when

Kittens Are Born Blind

House cats are able to produce three litters in a year. After a pregnancy of about nine weeks, the female gives birth to from three to five kittens. In rare cases, she gives birth to as many as eight. The pregnant female seeks out a safe hiding place when she senses that the kittens are ready to be born. She will typically choose an empty cardboard box in the attic or a dark corner of a haystack. Here the kittens, born blind and completely helpless, will be protected from the elements, such as the cold or wind, during their first few weeks of life. If the mother is concerned about any harm coming to the newborns during these first weeks, she will carry the kittens one by one to another area that seems safer. The tiny kittens weigh only about 3.5 ounces (100 g) at birth. They grow very rapidly because of the high protein content of their

more than one male shows interest in a female. These fights leave the males with torn ears, scratched noses, and bitten paws. This does not change the affection that the male and female have for one another. Fighting between males is just as much a traditional part of the mating ritual as howling.

The mating lasts for only a few seconds. Afterward, the female often turns against the male, hissing and scratching. The female wants the male to leave her alone as soon as possible. It is not clear why the female behaves this way toward her companion, but the tomcat doesn't seem to mind. He shows no interest in parental responsibility.

Russian Blue **Carthusian** **Rex Devon** **Burmese**

mother's milk. The kittens open their eyes when they are nine or ten days old. The period that follows is difficult for the mother because the kittens are active and constantly getting into some sort of trouble. The mother shows great patience in trying to let her kittens do whatever they please, as she untiringly keeps them from harm.

Sometime after the fourth week, the mother begins to teach her offspring how to hunt. She brings live mice to them and lets them practice pouncing on these mice. At first, the mice slip away from the clumsy little kittens. In time, however, the kittens increase their skill. They learn how to catch the mice with astonishing speed. Soon, the playful young cats are accomplished hunters.

A little later, the youngsters go out into the wild to hunt with their mother. At first, they hunt for only a few minutes, but after a while, they hunt for longer periods of time. While on these hunting trips, the kittens are gradually introduced by their mothers to all the various prey animals. The kittens learn how to conduct themselves properly while stalking. Soon, they have mastered all the tricks of the trade and are able to go out hunting alone. Finally, when they are six or seven months old, they leave their mother and strike out completely on their own. They will spend their approximately fifteen eventful years of life sometimes as a cuddly pet and sometimes as an independent wild animal.

Persian Colorpoint **Abyssinian** **Persian Red-shaded Cameo** **Siamese**

European wild cat

jungle cat

sand cat

African black-footed cat

Pallas' cat

serval

A Guide to Small Cats

Cats not pictured here:
bobcat, caracal, and Asiatic golden cat

lynx

African golden cat

leopard cat

rusty-spotted cat

fishing cat

flat-headed cat

marbled cat

jaguarundi

ocelot

margay

's cat

pampas cat

house cat

puma

clouded leopard

15

Wild Cats

Total length: 22-32 inches (50-80 cm)
Tail length: 10-16 inches (25-40 cm)
Weight: 7-18 pounds (3-8 kg)

African wild cat

Asian wild cat

Wild cats live throughout Europe, Africa, and both South and Central Asia. Within this vast territory, three different types of wild cats can be found.

The wild cats of Europe and the Near East are called wood cats. At first glance, they look like tiger-striped house cats. One typical characteristic of the wood cats is a bushy tail with dark rings and a blunt, dark tip. The tail is relatively short compared to that of a house cat. In addition, wood cats are about one-third the size of house cats, with the males being considerably larger than the females. This is true for all types of cats.

African and Arabian wild cats are called dun cats. These include, among others, the Nubian dun cat. The Nubian dun cat lives in North Africa and is the ancestor of house cats. Dun cats are usually smaller than wood cats, and their striped markings appear to be more faded.

Asian wild cats are known as steppe cats. Generally, they also are smaller than wood cats. Their coats are not striped, however. Instead, their fur is spotted.

Central European wood cats are quiet and mysterious inhabitants of the forest. These cats are only rarely seen, and they spend their days resting on boulders, on tree stumps, or on a sturdy branch. From these locations, they can enjoy a good overview of their surroundings. If there is the least disturbance, they will dive into the undergrowth near the ground and hide. As all cats typically do, the wood cat will become more active toward evening, going into the woods and the surrounding fields in search of prey. The main source of food for the wood cat is rodents, including everything from mice to rats to squirrels. Wood cats are also fond of birds. Occasionally, they will eat a young rabbit or a fawn.

Only recently, wood cats almost disappeared from Central Europe. In fact, they nearly became extinct because of ruthless hunters everywhere. It is mainly because of the cats' natural shyness that they have been able to survive. But today, conditions seem better for the wood cat in Central Europe. Ever since it was declared an endangered species in Germany and in Switzerland, its numbers have steadily increas

Opposite: European wild cats search

Jungle Cats

Total length: 22-38 inches (56-94 cm)
Tail length: 8-12 inches (20-31 cm)
Weight: 11-26.5 pounds (5-12 kg)

The jungle cat can be found from Egypt all across southern Asia as far as Indochina. It usually lives near rivers and lakes in thickets, in swampy woods along riverbanks, and in reed banks or fields of high grass.

There is a tuft of black hair about .5 inches (1.5 cm) long on the tips of the jungle cat's ears. This marking is also typical of the lynx, so the jungle cat, which often lives in swampy areas, is sometimes called the "swamp lynx."

The jungle cat is a skilled hunter that preys most frequently on water birds of all kinds, as well as pheasants, partridges, and peacocks. It is not afraid to live near humans, and it sometimes helps itself to chickens from a farm. Naturally, the jungle cat is not very popular with farmers because of this intrusion on their livestock. Naturalist T. C. Jerdon recorded his experience with a jungle cat in nineteenth-century India: "When I shot a peahen on the edge of a sugarcane field, one of these cats suddenly sprang out of nowhere, snatched up the dead hen, and disappeared back into the undergrowth — without stopping to say 'thank you:'"

In ancient Egyptian wall drawings, a wood cat can occasionally be seen alongside the African wild cat and the lion. The ancient Egyptians valued the jungle cat as a loyal and helpful hunting companion. If a bird that had been hunted down fell into an impassable thicket, the tame and well-trained jungle cat could easily fetch it.

A jungle cat crouches warily even as it drinks from a puddle of water.

Sand Cats

Total length: 15.5-22 inches (39-55 cm)
Tail length: 9-13.5 inches (23-34 cm)
Weight: 3-7 pounds (1.3-3 kg)

A sand cat hisses its disapproval.

The sand cat is a typical desert animal that lives in the deserts of Africa, the Arabian Peninsula, and the Middle East.

The sand cat is well adapted to the conditions of desert life. It has a thick pad of fur under its paws, made up of the long hair around and between the balls of its feet. With these "felt slippers" the little desert cat can move with ease and comfort across the open surface of sand. Anyone who has ever walked barefoot over burning sand can imagine how important this feature is to the sand cat.

Other adaptations to its desolate habitat include the sand cat's broad, flat skull, and ears that lie far back on the sides of its head. Since plants to hide behind are scarce in the desert, the distinctive shape of its head allows the sand cat to make itself flat. This way, even a slight unevenness of the sand dunes can serve as a hiding place.

The sand cat most often eats small desert rodents, lizards, and insects.

African Black-footed Cats

Total length: 17-20 inches (43-50 cm)
Tail length: 6-8.5 inches (15-22 cm)
Weight: 3-6 pounds (1.5-3 kg)

An African black-footed cat crouches tensely.

The African black-footed cat is the smallest of all the cats. Compared to the house cat, it looks much smaller, and it has even been crossbred with the domestic cat. The tiny black-footed cats are at home in the Karoo and the Kalahari, two desertlike dry plains in Southern Africa. These cats have sand-colored coats with spots that sometimes form into stripes.

The black-footed cat is a close relative of the North African sand cat. Like the sand cat, it has a broad skull with low-set ears and protective pads of hair on its feet. The pads and the soles of its feet are black. This is how the cat gets its name.

The South African Masarwa have great respect for the small black-footed cat.

A third desert cat related to both the sand and black-footed cats is the gray cat, also known as the Chinese desert cat. It lives in the dry plains and semidesert areas of China, Tibet, and Mongolia.

Pallas' Cats

Total length: 20-25.5 inches (50-65 cm)
Tail length: 8-12 inches (21-31 cm)
Weight: 5.5-10 pounds (2.5-4.5 kg)

the Pallas' cat curls up for a nap, it looks like a round fur pillow. It wraps its bushy tail around its paws as protection from the cold.

Scientists have made a recent discovery about the Pallas' cat. When hunting, it is able to observe prey using only the upper half of a

Each hair in the Pallas' cat's long, silver-gray coat is black at the tip and white in the middle.

The Pallas' cat lives on the plains, rocky wastelands, and treeless cliffs of the highlands of Central Asia, from Afghanistan as far as Mongolia. In some places, the Pallas' cat will live as high as 9,850-13,125 feet (3,000-4,000 m) in the mountains.

The Pallas' cat is well adapted to the raw climate in which it lives. The wind blows constantly, and the winter cold is bitter. The hair of the cat's coat is long and thick. When

single eye. It may be the cat's strangely-shaped pupils that allow it to do this. The pupils do not come together in a slit like those of most other cats. Instead, they form a shape that is a cross between a circle and a rectangle.

The main source of meals for the Pallas' cats are the guinea-pig-like relatives of the rabbit that live in the high Asian mountains between the rocks. The Pallas' cat will also feed on rodents and prairie birds.

Servals

Total length: 27.5-39 inches (70-100 cm)
Tail length: 12-16 inches (30-40 cm)
Weight: 15.5-40 pounds (7-18 kg)

No other cat has ears as large as those of the serval, which lives south of the Sahara in Africa's savannas. Its ears are funnel-shaped, and the inner edges come together on the cat's forehead. These ears give the serval an exceptional sense of hearing.

When hunting, the serval easily glides through thick plant growth — tall grass as high as a person's shoulder. The serval's ears are a great advantage in this environment. They can detect even the tiniest sounds, such as the rustling of a rodent or the scratching noises made by a bird on the ground. The cat can then slink along unseen until it is near the source of the sound and surprise its prey. The serval will frequently stun rodents with two or three hard blows from its front paws before killing them with a single bite.

The serval's front paws are another striking physical feature. They are extremely long and mobile, and the serval can use them to search for prey in rodent holes. It feels around for inhabitants hiding in the holes, then grabs them securely with its claws and pulls them out of the hole. The serval's sensitive hearing is useful here as well. It can actually hear animals crawling in their burrows underground and can tell when it is time to reach into a hole.

Young servals spend the first few weeks of life well hidden in an abandoned groundhog burrow, between boulders, or in dense underbrush. At the end of this time, they emerge with their mother to explore the world.

The serval's large ears enable it to hear better than other cats. The ears are black on the outside, with a bright, white spot in the middle.

21

Lynxes

Total length: 31.5-51 inches (80-130 cm)
Tail length: 4-10 inches (10-25 cm)
Weight: 33-84 pounds (15-38 kg)

fallen trees. The plentiful plant life provides ample cover for hunting prey. The lynx's most frequent prey are fawns, hares, prairie chickens, and common partridges. If the lynx is extremely hungry, it will also eat mice, lizards, frogs, beetles, and other small animals. However, the lynx prefers to eat

The lynx leads a solitary life. It hunts mainly at night, using its keen senses of sight and smell.

The lynx is a long-legged cat with a stubby tail. It has noticeable tufts of fur at the tips of its ears, pointed sideburns, and a brown speckled coat. It lives primarily in the northern regions of Europe, Asia, and North America. The winters in these regions are often long and hard, but the lynx doesn't seem to mind. Its heavy coat protects the lynx against even the most bitter cold. With its huge, broad paws covered with thick fur, it can walk on even the softest snow without sinking very deeply. These paws act as snowshoes.

The lynx is a forest cat. It prefers to live in aging forests with thick undergrowth and

larger animals because it does not need to catch as many of them to satisfy its hunger.

In Central Europe, people once hunted the lynx mercilessly, either because they felt the cat was a pest or because they were simply afraid of this predator. Recently, however, people have changed their attitude toward the lynx; they are finally beginning to realize that there is enough room on this planet for all people and animals. Because of this change of heart, the long-legged hunter has successfully made itself at home again over the past twenty years in Germany, Austria, France, and Switzerland.

Bobcats

Total length: 24.5-37.5 inches (62-95 cm)
Tail length: 5-7.5 inches (13-19 cm)
Weight: 9-41 pounds (4-18.5 kg)

The bobcat looks a lot like the lynx, but the bobcat is a smaller animal, and the tip of its tail is a different color. The tip of the bobcat's tail is white; the tip of the lynx's tail is black.

The bobcat lives in North America, and it can be found in a wide range of terrain. It lives on the bush-covered cliffs of the Rocky Mountains, the humid, swampy woods of Florida, and the cactus thickets of the Mexican desert. These cats have even been spotted on the outskirts of big cities.

The bobcat is not fussy when it comes to food. Just about anything that crawls or flies is fair game for this skilled hunter. The bobcat eats everything from flies and beetles to fawns that weigh several times as much as the cat. Bobcats have even been spotted in caves, trying to catch bats.

Although the bobcat was once hunted for its beautiful pelt, its numbers are still plentiful. In the United States alone, there are more than one million bobcats.

Bobcat kittens rest in a cool, shady spot.

Caracals

Total length: 24.5-32 inches (62-82 cm)
Tail length: 9-12.5 inches (23-32 cm)
Weight: 17.5-40 pounds (8-18 kg)

The caracal likes a dry climate. It inhabits the deserts, semideserts, and arid savannas of Africa, Arabia, and the Near East. The caracal is frequently referred to as the desert lynx. The name caracal stems from a Turkish word and means "black ear." This is because the backs of its ears are black in color.

The caracal is a skilled bird hunter. It is also one of the most powerful high-jumpers among the small cats. It can leap 10 feet (3 m) into the air from a standing position. It can even jump straight upward and snatch a low-flying guinea hen in midair.

In days past in India and the Near East, the caracal was trained to hunt for antelope, rabbits, and pheasants. The skill of a trained caracal was often measured by how many pigeons it could catch from a flock pecking at the ground before the birds had time to fly away. According to some legends, a good hunting caracal could catch as many as ten to twelve pigeons.

A caracal warily surveys its terrain.

Asiatic Golden Cats

Total length: 29.5-41.5 inches (75-105 cm)
Tail length: 19-22 inches (49-56 cm)
Weight: 15.5-33 pounds (7-15 kg)

Asiatic golden cat

The Asiatic golden cat, often referred to as Temminck's cat, is similar to the African golden cat. Like the latter, the Asiatic golden cat lives in forests. Some of these cats are red in color, and some are gray. Some have solid-colored coats, and some have spotted coats.

The Bornean red cat, or bay cat, is a miniature version of the Asiatic golden cat, with a total length of 20-24 inches (50-60 cm). It is found only on the island of Borneo.

African Golden Cats

Total length: 25.5-37.5 inches (65-95 cm)
Tail length: 11-16 inches (28-40 cm)
Weight: 22-37.5 pounds (10-17 kg)

The African golden cat lives in the dark, humid forests of equatorial Africa between Senegal in the west and Kenya in the east and in the lush vegetation of the areas just north of them.

The African golden cat is often referred to as a "master of disguise" because its appearance varies so greatly. Its coat can be an entire range of colors, from red to cinnamon, chocolate brown, slate gray, or even pitch black. The markings on the golden cat's coat also vary. Some of these cats have coats that are nearly solid in color; others have coats with clearly defined spots. The spotted cats are most frequently found in the western part of their territorial range.

Little is known about how the African golden cat lives in the wild. Some experts say it spends its days sleeping in the branch of a forest tree. Most likely, it begins to stir around twilight and spends the night hunting on the ground. Its prey consists of all types of small animals.

Many African tribes have great respect for the golden cat and say they appear in different "clothes." Native peoples tell wonderful stories about the golden cat. The Liberians, for example, believe the golden cat is the full brother of the leopard; they both fear and honor this cat more than other animals. The Pygmies of the Congo Basin believe the golden cat's tail is a lucky charm that brings success during dangerous elephant hunts.

This African golden cat sits ready for action in its lush, tropical habitat. It may be warning unwelc⟨ trespassers of its presence.

Leopard Cats

Total length: 16-36 inches (40-90 cm)
Tail length: 6-14.5 inches (15-37 cm)
Weight: 6.5-18 pounds (3-8 kg)

Philippines are dark and very small. Alfred Brehm, the "father of animal study," wrote about the leopard cat about one hundred years ago: ". . . it is among the wildest and most rapacious animals of its species." Indeed, the courage and cunning shown by these beautiful animals are greater than many much larger cats. Their prey animals include

These adorable leopard kittens will soon be ferocious hunters.

The leopard cat lives in the bushy or forested areas of Southeast Asia, between the Amur River in the north, the Indus River in the west, and the island of Java in the south. The coloring, markings, and body size of the leopard cat vary according to where it comes from. This is often the case for animals that live across such a broad range of territory. The biggest and most brightly colored leopard cats are from Manchuria. Those from the

pheasants, rabbits, and even small deer. They also prey on smaller animals. The leopard cat will fearlessly enter barns and stables owned by farmers; sheep and chickens are not safe from the leopard cat.

The Iriomote cat is closely related to the leopard cat. It was first discovered in 1967 on the Japanese island of Iriomote. It is one of the rarest small cats. There are only about forty cats of its kind.

Rusty-spotted Cats

Total length: 14-19 inches (35-48 cm)
Tail length: 6-10 inches (15-25 cm)
Weight: approximately 4.5 pounds (2 kg)

The rusty-spotted cat begins its hunt at twilight.

forests in the southern part of the island instead of the dry areas in the north.

Like all small cats, the rusty-spotted cat sharpens its claws on certain "scratching posts" within its territory. This behavior does more than simply keep its claws sharpened. The rusty-spotted cat uses the opportunity of scratching to leave signals behind for other

The rusty-spotted cat, sometimes called the rust cat, is so named because of its beautiful rust-colored coat. This cat lives in southern India and on the island of Sri Lanka.

Strangely, the rusty-spotted cats that live in southern India favor a different habitat than those in nearby Sri Lanka. In India, the animals prefer to stalk through dry grasslands and brush and avoid the dense woods. On Sri Lanka, they prefer the humid mountain rain

cats. These signals are distinctive scents produced by the well-designed sweat glands found between the soles of the cat's feet. Therefore, tree-scratching and urine marks serve to inform other cats of the rusty-spotted cat's comings and goings.

The rusty-spotted cat is a nocturnal hunter; that is, it prefers to stalk its prey animals at night. It eats small mammals, birds, lizards, and insects.

Fishing Cats

Total length: 27.5-34 inches (70-86 cm)
Tail length: 10-13 inches (25-33 cm)
Weight: 17.5-33 pounds (8-15 kg)

swim by. When a fish finally comes within reach, the cat will snatch it from the water with one lightning-fast sweep of its front paw — the same way house cats might fish for goldfish in an aquarium.

In its search for prey, the fishing cat will often wade in the standing water in the swamp, catching insects, frogs, small

The brownish gray fur of the fishing cat is short and coarse.

No other small cat has such close links to the water as the fishing cat. In its home on the Southeast Asian mainland and the islands of Sri Lanka, Sumatra, and Java, it always lives very close to water. It also lives in swamplands and wooded shoreline areas, in reeds along rivers and streams, in mangrove thickets, and in sandy marshes along the seacoast.

As its name implies, the fishing cat is a talented catcher of fish. It loves to crouch along a bank and patiently wait for a fish to

mammals, and all sorts of birds. Just how well-adapted the fishing cat is to life in and around the water can be illustrated by the fact that webbing can be found between the toes on its paws.

The fishing cat hides inside hollow trees, between boulders, and in other safe places. After a pregnancy of about sixty-three days, the female gives birth to two or three kittens that weigh only 6 ounces (170 g) at birth and are 7 inches (18 cm) long.

Flat-headed Cats

Total length: 18-24 inches (45-61 cm)
Tail length: 5-8 inches (12-20 cm)
Weight: 4.5-11 pounds (2-5 kg)

The flat-headed cat is a mystery among the small cats of the Old World. Next to nothing is known about its habits in the wild. The reason for this lack of knowledge is the extraordinary rareness of the flat-headed cat.

The native inhabitants of Borneo have observed that the flat-headed cat likes fruit and will even dig up sweet potatoes from

The mysterious flat-headed cat is mainly nocturnal and hunts fish and frogs.

The flat-headed cat lives on the Malayan Peninsula and the islands of Borneo and Sumatra. It differs from its Southeast Asian relatives in some of its physical characteristics. For example, unlike its relatives, it has an especially flat-topped skull. This, of course, accounts for its name. Also, its coat has only a few markings, and its eyes are unusually large and dark. Finally, the flat-headed cat has an unusual bite — many of its teeth are pointed.

gardens. It tears the potatoes open, loudly smacking its lips. This would seem to fit the image of this unusual cat, but many cat specialists think that the flat-headed cat does not eat fruit or potatoes after all. They believe that the flat-headed cat, like the fishing cat, lives near water and catches fish, frogs, and crabs. The cat's pointed teeth would seem to indicate that this is true. Animals usually have pointed teeth in order to catch and secure slippery prey.

Marbled Cats

Total length: 18-24 inches (45-61 cm)
Tail length: 14-21 inches (35-54 cm)
Weight: 9-18 pounds (4-8 kg)

The marbled cat is a ferocious predator.

The marbled cat inhabits the ancient forests of Southeast Asia. It does not like to live near humans and lives only in undisturbed forests far away from civilization. Such areas are growing increasingly rare, so the population of marbled cats is constantly decreasing.

Little is known about the marbled cat. In fact, this cat was once thought to be a type of clouded leopard. Except for the South American margay cat, the marbled cat appears to be the only small cat that likes to live in trees. There it hunts for birds, squirrels, and other small animals.

The marbled cat gets its name from its coat, which looks like a boldly patterned slab of marble. Its fur is very soft and long, and the coat pattern varies from one animal to another. It usually carries its tail in a loosely curled position. The marbled cat is considered by experts to be very ferocious.

Jaguarundis

Total length: 22-30 inches (55-77 cm)
Tail length: 13-23 inches (33-60 cm)
Weight: 11-20 pounds (5-9 kg)

Of all the small cats, the jaguarundi looks least like a cat. With its long body, short legs, dark, solidly-colored pelt and small, rounded ears, it looks more like an otter, a marten, or a weasel. The jaguarundi has one other unusual feature. Its pupils, which are completely round, come together to form a small pin-hole when they close.

Jaguarundis come in two colors. One variety is grayish brown or black; the other ranges from reddish brown to chestnut brown. At one time, cats with light-shaded coats were thought to make up a completely different species, called *eyra*. But experts have discovered this is not the case. Jaguarundis of both types can be born in the same litter.

The jaguarundi lives in wooded and bushy areas of Central and South America. When these cats hunt, they prefer extended bushy plains and the bushy areas around forests to either the forest itself or open land. With their streamlined shape, they are well adapted to living in thick brush and are agile in this kind of terrain. The chief prey animals of these cats are all kinds of birds and small mammals like rabbits and guinea pigs.

Ancient records state that the Indians of Central and South America often tamed jaguarundis and kept the cats in their huts. The cats kept rats and mice away, but no one knows for sure if the Indians were also able to train the jaguarundis to leave their domestic chickens alone.

Opposite: Although the jaguarundi lives mainly in forest areas, it also inhabits swampy areas and is an excellent swimmer.

Ocelots

Total length: 27.5-40 inches (70-100 cm)
Tail length: 10.5-18 inches (27-45 cm)
Weight: 24-35 pounds (11-16 kg)

The ocelot lives throughout Central and South America. It is at home in a variety of habitats — in warm, humid jungles, foggy mountain forests, flooded mangrove thickets, and semiarid thornbush savannas. The only areas it never inhabits are open fields; it prefers bush and forest country.

Although a skilled climber, the ocelot hunts mainly on the ground. Nighttime prowls cover a territory that averages between 2-4 miles (3-6 km). The ocelot will hunt prey of all sizes — from mice and frogs to turtles and birds, all the way to small deer and wild pigs. There have even been reports of an ocelot killing an 8-foot (2.5-m) python.

The ocelot has one of the most beautiful coats in the world. Its spotted pattern serves as camouflage in the underbrush so the cat can approach its prey without being noticed.

This camouflage has ironically endangered the ocelot. In the 1960s, coats made of wild cat fur came into fashion, and the demand for ocelot pelts was enormous. In 1969, as many as 133,070 ocelot pelts were imported into the United States from South America. The beautiful cat soon became extinct in many of its natural habitats. Fortunately, recent legal restrictions against hunting wild animals and selling their pelts seem to have had a positive effect on the ocelot population. But the small, spotted cat is again threatened by the human destruction of its South American forest homes.

Opposite: The ocelot's beautifully patterned coat unfortunately makes this animal valuable to the fur trade.

Margays

Total length: 18-31 inches (46-79 cm)
Tail length: 13-20 inches (33-51 cm)
Weight: 6.5-20 pounds (3-9 kg)

The agile margay only rarely hunts on the ground.

The margay is a forest cat that can be found all across Central and South America. Many people also refer to it as the "tree ocelot." This makes sense because the animal lives almost exclusively in the branches of trees. It climbs around in the trees with the grace and skill of an acrobat. The margay can run up a tree in a spiral movement and hang by four legs from a branch. It can also hang from a branch by only one leg, or climb down a tree head first like a squirrel — all without any great effort. It can perform all these tricks with the help of its long tail, which serves to help the cat balance its body.

The margay spends most of the day sleeping in a hollow tree or hidden among the leaves. It spends the night in the treetops hunting for squirrels, opossums, monkeys, birds, and tree frogs.

Geoffroy's Cats

Total length: about 36 inches (91 cm)
Tail length: 10-14 inches (25-35 cm)
Weight: 9-17.5 pounds (4-8 kg)

offspring. They function as reflectors, making it easy for the young cats to see their mother in the dense undergrowth during a hunt.

The basic coloring of the Geoffroy's cat varies greatly. In the northern part of its territorial range, it can be a light yellow; in the south, it can be a silvery gray. In all cases, the coat is covered with a fine flecked pattern,

The Geoffroy's cat is an excellent climber. It often uses this ability to drop on unsuspecting prey.

Another South American small cat is the Geoffroy's cat, which can be found all the way from Bolivia in the north to Patagonia in the south. It prefers to live in semi-open terrain with plenty of rocks and brush. Here it hunts mostly for small rodents such as mice, rats, guinea pigs, and agoutis. Like many other small cats, Geoffroy's cat has ears that are black on the back with one white spot in the center. These noticeable markings play an important part in the raising of the cat's

and the tail is covered with twelve to sixteen dark rings. Unfortunately, fur dealers place great value on the animal's coat, and the cat is frequently hunted.

The Chilean forest cat, or kodkod cat, inhabits the southernmost part of South America and is closely related to the Geoffroy's cat. This cat is also covered with spots. It is one of the dwarfs in the cat family, with an overall total length of only 15.5-20.5 inches (39-52 cm).

Pampas Cats

Total length: 21-27.5 inches (53-70 cm)
Tail length: 10.5-14 inches (27-35 cm)
Weight: 9-15.5 pounds (4-7 kg)

A striking feature of the pampas cat is the long hair on its back. The hair sometimes measures up to 2.5 inches (7 cm) in length. The cat raises this hair when it senses danger. The hair on its thighs is also long and spreads out when the animal is excited. If the pampas cat also shows its teeth and hisses, it makes a frightening impression. It was this sight

This fierce little pampas cat detects a rustling movement in the nearby brush.

The pampas cat makes its home in the southern part of South America. Its preferred territory is the high grass of the open, treeless prairies called the *pampas*. This, of course, is how the cat received its name.

When making its rounds through the thick, high grass, the pampas cat moves forward in short, hurried steps, almost as if it were trotting. It likes to hunt for tinamous and other partridge-like birds of the pampas. This beautiful cat is about the size of a house cat.

that inspired the naturalist Juan I. Molina to give the pampas cat the scientific name *colocolo* in 1782. Colocolo was the name of a feared Chilean Indian chieftain.

The mountain cat looks very much like the pampas cat, but it has an especially thick coat and an extremely long, bushy tail. The mountain cat lives in South America in the steep, rocky cliffs of the High Andes, sometimes in areas at altitudes as high as 16,400 feet (5,000 m).

Pumas

Total length: 41.5-71 inches (105-180 cm)
Tail length: 24-35.5 inches (60-90 cm)
Weight: 77-220 pounds (35-100 kg)

A puma cub fondly licks its mother.

The puma is the giant among the small cats. In terms of size and weight, it is similar to two types of big cats — the leopard and the jaguar. Like these cats, the puma's pupils close into a circular shape. But in every other way, the puma is a proper small cat, and there is no doubt it belongs to this family.

The puma's territorial range is also large. It is found throughout North, Central, and South America. It is every bit as much at home in woods as it is in grasslands, deserts, and high mountains. This big small cat is not particular about its surroundings other than there be enough prey animals and sufficient cover for hunting.

The puma almost always hunts at night. It eats almost all the animals found in its habitat, from grasshoppers to elk. Its main prey animals are deer of all types, but the puma also eats wild boar, rabbits, beaver, and prairie dogs. Even coyotes, skunks, and porcupines have to watch out for the puma, as well as sea lions in South America. Attacks on humans by this cat are extremely rare because the puma is very shy.

People once thought the puma had a negative effect on the deer population, but this is not true. The puma most often kills deer that are sick or injured, since these animals are much easier to kill. In this way, the puma actually makes an important contribution toward keeping the deer population healthy.

Pumas are loners that usually remain loyal to one hunting territory for their entire lifetime. The size of this territory depends on the availability of prey animals. The territory averages about 19 square miles (50 sq. km) for males and somewhat less for females. During mating season, males and females travel and sleep side by side and even hunt together. However, they separate before the birth of their offspring since the male does not take on any fatherly responsibilities.

After a pregnancy of about three months, the female gives birth to two or three cubs. At birth, the baby pumas are only 8-12 inches (20-30 cm) long and weigh only 8-16 ounces (230-450 g). Newborn pumas have spotted coats that begin to fade when the cubs are about two months old. The spots fully disappear by the time the cat is six months old. The young cats remain with their mother

The powerful puma is also called a cougar or a mountain lion in the United States and Canada.

for approximately twenty months. During that time, she introduces them to the art of hunting. Pumas need a lot more time to reach maturity than young house cats. It takes pumas a relatively long period of time before they are able to hunt and survive in the wild on their own. Nonetheless, the life expectation of a puma is no longer than that of a house cat. Very few pumas live to be older than fifteen years of age.

Life became difficult for the American pumas with the arrival of European settlers. The puma did not know the difference between wild and domesticated animals and often attacked cattle, sheep, and goats. Because of overhunting by humans, the puma became rare in many parts of the Americas. But thanks to effective conservation measures undertaken during this century, the number of pumas has fortunately begun to rise.

Not a Small Cat, Not a Big Cat

Clouded Leopards

Total length: 30-41.5 inches (75-105 cm)
Tail length: 27.5-35.5 inches (70-90 cm)
Weight: 40-48.5 pounds (18-22 kg)

A clouded leopard snarls a warning to intruders.

The clouded leopard does not fit perfectly with either the big cats or the small ones. For example, it is nearly the size of a leopard. Therefore, it is one size too big for the small cats and one size too small for the big cats. Its pupils close in a spindle shape, which is different from both big and small cats. When at rest, the clouded leopard stretches its tail out straight behind it, as the big cats do. But the clouded leopard purrs like a small cat. Specialists have therefore created a special category for this exceptional cat — *Neofelis*.

The clouded leopard lives in the evergreen rain forests of Southeast Asia, as well as Sumatra, Java, Borneo, and Taiwan. Indonesians call the cat *harimau dahan*, or "tree branch tiger," because it spends most of its time high up in the trees. It can easily climb headfirst down a tree trunk, while most other cats have to climb down awkwardly, constantly looking backward over their shoulders. Because of its life in the trees, the clouded leopard has developed unusually long claws to help it maintain a firm hold on branches and tree trunks. Also, its long tail helps it keep its balance in the tree. Because of its short but muscular legs, the clouded leopard is able to jump distances of up to 16.5 feet (5 m) between two trees in one powerful leap. In addition, the cat's beautiful markings, which are pale and cloudy, provide it with excellent camouflage among the leaves.

During the day, the clouded leopard dozes lazily in the fork of a tree. It becomes more active in the evening when it goes out to stalk food. This master climber will catch all sorts of birds, squirrels, monkeys, and even young orangutans. But it also likes wild pigs, deer, and other ground mammals. The clouded leopard will sometimes lie in wait for its prey animals in the branch of a tree and suddenly leap down upon them. The cat will also stalk its prey from the ground. Its long, daggerlike teeth serve the cat well when it needs to hunt large animals.

Scientists have only a little information about the reproductive behavior of clouded leopards in the wild. In zoos, female clouded leopards give birth to from two to four cubs after a pregnancy of about three months. The cubs weigh 5-6 ounces (140-170 g) at birth. Like all newborn cats, they are blind at first, but open their eyes after ten or twelve days.

The cubs are weaned at about five months and are fully grown at eight or nine months. Clouded leopards have been known to live up to seventeen years in captivity.

Unfortunately, the clouded leopard population is diminishing because many Southeast Asian rain forests are being cut down to provide timber and clear land for human settlements. The International Union for the Protection of Nature has had to put the clouded leopard on its "red list" of endangered species. It is essential to the survival of the clouded leopard that as many tropical forests as possible are protected by law.

Although larger than the other members of its family, the clouded leopard still purrs like a small cat.

House Cats

This beautiful house cat seems ready to say "goodbye." It cannot actually speak as humans do, but the house cat does command an incredibly rich language of its own. It has more than fifty different sounds available to express its every mood and impulse. These sounds include the "meow" in all its variations. But cats can also make cooing, rasping, and cackling sounds; they can hiss, growl, screech, snarl, howl, and much more. Last but not least, house cats make an uninterrupted humming sound, called *purring*. Only small cats can purr — the big cats cannot.

Purring is the expression of a cat's feeling of contentment or well-being. Every sound a cat makes has its own meaning, so an attentive cat owner is sometimes able to delightfully converse with his or her house cat.

APPENDIX
TO
ANIMAL FAMILIES

SMALL CATS

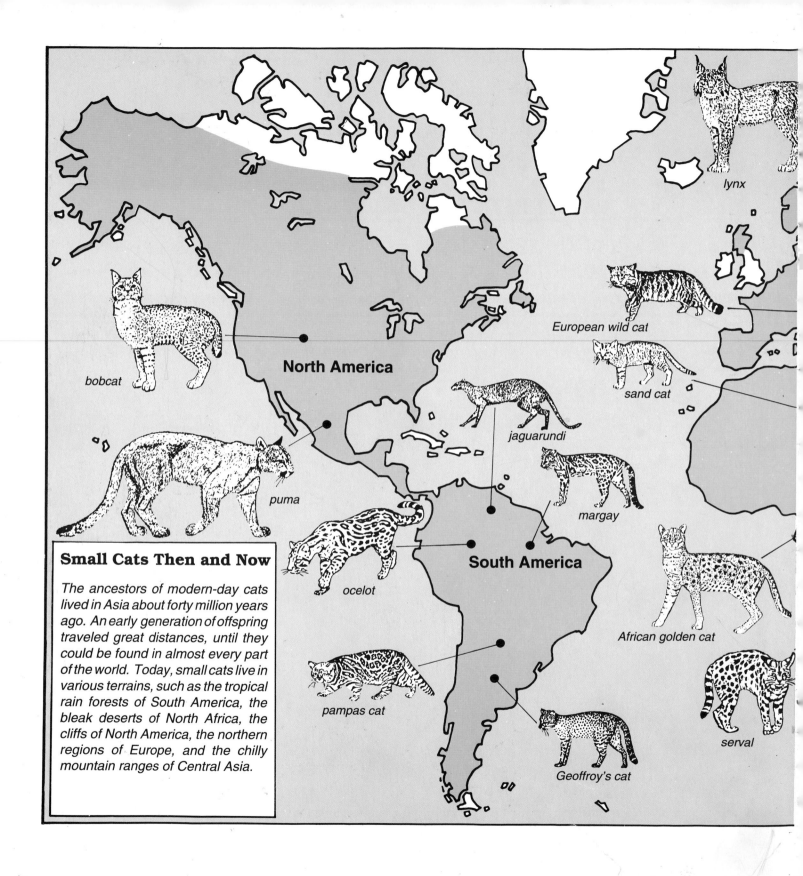

lynx

European wild cat

sand cat

bobcat

North America

puma

jaguarundi

margay

ocelot

South America

African golden cat

pampas cat

serval

Geoffroy's cat

Small Cats Then and Now

The ancestors of modern-day cats lived in Asia about forty million years ago. An early generation of offspring traveled great distances, until they could be found in almost every part of the world. Today, small cats live in various terrains, such as the tropical rain forests of South America, the bleak deserts of North Africa, the cliffs of North America, the northern regions of Europe, and the chilly mountain ranges of Central Asia.

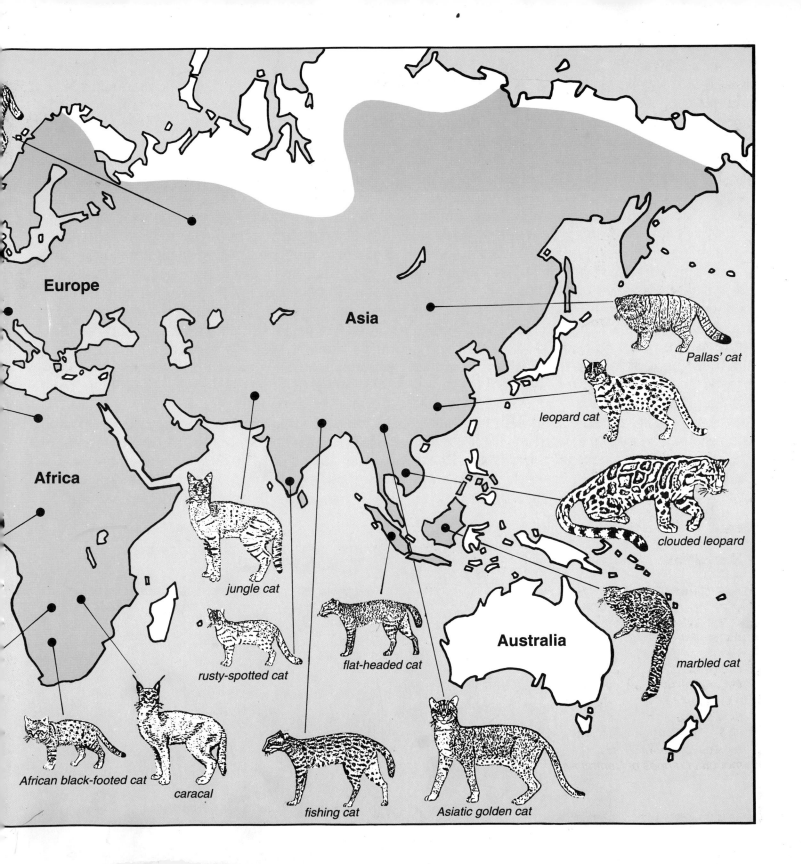

Europe

Asia

Africa

Australia

Pallas' cat

leopard cat

clouded leopard

marbled cat

jungle cat

rusty-spotted cat

flat-headed cat

African black-footed cat

caracal

fishing cat

Asiatic golden cat

ABOUT THESE BOOKS

Although this series is called "Animal Families," these books aren't just about fathers, mothers, and young. They also discuss the scientific definition of *family*, which is a division of biological classification and includes many animals.

Biological classification is a method that scientists use to identify and organize living things. Using this system, scientists place animals and plants into larger groups that share similar characteristics. Characteristics are physical features, natural habits, ancestral backgrounds, or any other qualities that make one organism either like or different from another.

The method used today for biological classification was introduced in 1753 by a Swedish botanist-naturalist named Carolus Linnaeus. Although many scientists tried to find ways to classify the world's plants and animals, Linnaeus's system seemed to be the only useful choice. Charles Darwin, a famous British naturalist, referred to Linnaeus's system in his theory of evolution, which was published in his book *On the Origin of Species* in 1859. Linnaeus's system of classification, shown below, includes seven major categories, or groups. These are: kingdom, phylum, class, order, family, genus, and species.

An easy way to remember the divisions and their order is to memorize this sentence: "Ken Put Cake On Frank's Good Shirt." The first letter of each word in this sentence gives you the first letter of a division. (The *K* in *Ken*, for example, stands for *kingdom*.) The order of the words in this sentence suggests the order of the divisions from largest to smallest. The kingdom is the largest of these divisions; the species is the smallest. The larger the division, the more types of animals or plants it contains. For example, the animal kingdom, called Animalia, contains everything from worms to whales. Smaller divisions, such as the family, have fewer members that share more characteristics. For example, members of the bear family, Ursidae, include the polar bear, the brown bear, and many others.

In the following chart, the lion species is followed through all seven categories. As the categories expand to include more and more members, remember that only a few examples are pictured here. Each division has many more members.

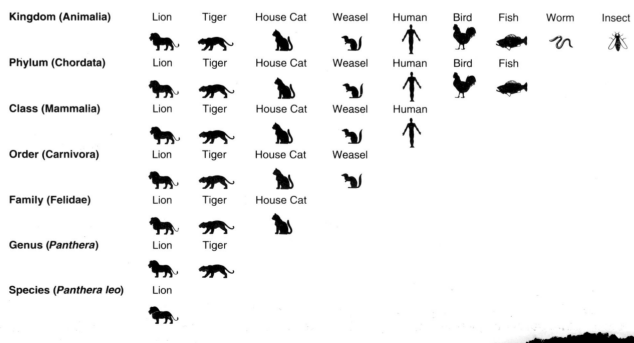

Kingdom (Animalia)	Lion	Tiger	House Cat	Weasel	Human	Bird	Fish	Worm	Insect
Phylum (Chordata)	Lion	Tiger	House Cat	Weasel	Human	Bird	Fish		
Class (Mammalia)	Lion	Tiger	House Cat	Weasel	Human				
Order (Carnivora)	Lion	Tiger	House Cat	Weasel					
Family (Felidae)	Lion	Tiger	House Cat						
Genus (*Panthera*)	Lion	Tiger							
Species (*Panthera leo*)	Lion								

SCIENTIFIC NAMES OF THE ANIMALS IN THIS BOOK

Animals have different names in every language. For this reason, researchers the world over use the same scientific names, which usually stem from ancient Greek or Latin. Most animals are classified by two names. One is the genus name; the other is the name of the species to which they belong. Additional names indicate further subgroupings. Here is a list of the animals included in *Small Cats*.

African golden cat .... *Felis aurata*
Asiatic golden cat (Temminck's cat) .... *Felis temmincki*
Leopard cat .... *Felis bengalensis*
Mountain cat .... *Felis jacobita*
Borneo cat (Bay cat) .... *Felis badia*
Chilean forest cat (Kodkod cat) .... *Felis guigna*
Fishing cat .... *Felis viverrina*
Flat-headed cat .... *Felis planiceps*
Chinese desert cat .... *Felis bieti*
House cat .... *Felis catus*
Iriomote cat .... *Felis iriomotensis*
Geoffroy's cat .... *Felis geoffroyi*
Margay .... *Felis wiedi*
Pallas' cat .... *Felis manul*
Marbled cat .... *Felis marmorata*

Lynx .... *Felis lynx*
Ocelot .... *Felis pardalis*
Pampas cat .... *Felis colocolo*
Puma .... *Felis concolor*
Jungle cat .... *Felis chaus*
Rusty-spotted cat .... *Felis rubiginosa*
Bobcat .... *Felis rufa*
Sand cat .... *Felis Margarita*
African black-footed cat .... *Felis nigripes*
Serval .... *Felis serval*
Jaguarundi .... *Felis yagouaroundi*
European wild cat .... *Felis silvestris*
Caracal .... *Felis caracal*
Clouded leopard .... *Neofelis nebulosa*

GLOSSARY

camouflage
The way an animal changes its appearance, hides, or disguises itself to look like its surroundings. Animals camouflage themselves both as a way of protecting themselves and as a way of sneaking up on their prey.

class
The third of seven divisions in the biological classification system proposed by Swedish botanist-naturalist Carolus Linnaeus. The class is the main subdivision of the phylum. Cats belong to the class Mammalia. Animals in this class, which includes humans, share certain features: they have skin covered with hair, they give birth to live young, and they nourish the young with milk from mammary glands.

cubs
The young of certain meat-eating animals. Pumas usually give birth to two or three cubs at one time.

domesticated
Tame; trained to live with and be useful to humans. Domesticated dun cats traveled from the Middle East to China and Europe thousands of years ago.

embalm
To prevent the decay of a corpse by special treatment with preservatives. Ancient Egyptians embalmed their cats and buried them in special cemeteries because cats were regarded as sacred.

endangered species
A group of animals that have become rare and are threatened with extinction, usually because of human behavior or a change in environmental conditions.

extinction
The condition of a species being completely destroyed or killed off.

family
The fifth of seven divisions in the biological classification system proposed by Swedish botanist-naturalist Carolus Linnaeus. A family is the main subdivision of the order and contains one or more genera. Cats belong to the family Felidae.

genus (plural: **genera**)
The sixth division in the biological classification system

proposed by Swedish botanist-naturalist Carolus Linnaeus. A genus is the main subdivision of a family and includes one or more species.

gestation period
The number of days from actual conception to the birth of an animal. Gestation periods vary greatly for different types of animals.

habitat
The natural living area or environment in which an animal usually lives.

interbreed
To mate with another kind or species. At one point in history, dun cats interbred with wild cats. That is why many present-day farm cats look like wild cats.

kingdom
The first of seven divisions in the biological classification system proposed by Swedish botanist-naturalist Carolus Linnaeus. Animals, including humans, belong to the kingdom Animalia. It is one of five kingdoms.

litter
All the young produced at one time by an animal. The size of a cat's litter depends on its species.

mammal
A warm-blooded animal that nurses its young with its own milk. Whales, humans, and cats are some examples of mammals.

mate (verb)
To join together (animals) to produce offspring. A house cat will give up its life as a loner when it feels the urge to mate.

nocturnal
Active at night and usually asleep during the day.

order
The fourth of seven divisions in the biological classification system proposed by the Swedish botanist-naturalist Carolus Linnaeus. The order is the main subdivision of the class and contains many different families. Cats belong to the order Carnivora. This order includes other meat-eating animal families.

pampas
Open, treeless range areas in South America.

pelt
The skin of an animal with the fur or hair still on it. Animal pelts are used to make coats and other articles of clothing.

phylum (plural: **phyla**)
The second of seven divisions in the biological classification system proposed by the Swedish botanist-naturalist Carolus Linnaeus. A phylum is one of the main divisions of a kingdom. Cats belong to the phylum Chordata, the group consisting mainly of animals with backbones (vertebrates).

predator
An animal that lives by eating other animals. All the small cats discussed in this book are predators.

prey
Any creature that is hunted or caught as food. A cat extends its claws when reaching for prey.

pupil
The opening in the eye's iris. In bright light, the pupils of most small cats close to form a narrow slit, thus protecting their delicate eyes from too much light.

savanna
A type of tropical or subtropical prairie. Some ocelots live in the semiarid thornbush savannas of Central and South America.

species
The last of seven divisions in the biological classification system proposed by Swedish botanist-naturalist Carolus Linnaeus. The species is the main subdivision of the genus. It may include further subgroups of its own, called subspecies. At the level of species, members share many features and are capable of breeding with one another. There are thirty-six species of cats worldwide.

***tapetum lucidum* ("carpet of light")**
Reflective tissue behind the cat's retina. The tapetum lucidum is responsible for the way a cat's eyes seem to light up when it encounters bright light in the dark.

MORE BOOKS ABOUT SMALL CATS

Caring for Your Cat. Mark McPherson (Troll Associates)
A Cat's Body. Joanna Cole (William Morrow & Co.)
Cats. Anna Sproule and Michael Sproule (Franklin Watts)
Cats: Little Tigers in Your House. Linda McCarter Bridge (National Geographic Society)
The Cats. W.G. Conway, J.W. Waddick, J.G. Doherty (Time-Life Films)
Drawing Cats and Kittens. Paul Frame (Franklin Watts)
The Kids' Cat Book. Tomie DePaola (Holiday House)
The Wild Cats. Jerolyn Ann Nentl (Crestwood House)

PLACES TO WRITE

The following are some of the many organizations that exist to educate people about animals, promote the protection of animals, and encourage the conservation of their environments. Write to these organizations for more information about small cats, other animals, or animal concerns of interest to you. When you write, include your name, address, and age, and tell them clearly what you want to know. Don't forget to enclose a stamped, self-addressed envelope for a reply.

Animal Protection Institute
P.O. Box 22505
Sacramento, California 95822

Elsa Clubs of America
P.O. Box 4572
North Hollywood, California
               91617-0572

Student Action Corps for Animals
P.O. Box 15588
Washington, D.C.   20003

Wilfdlife Conservation International
New York Zoological Society
185th Street and Southern Boulevard
Bronx, New York   10460

Wildlife Preservation Trust International
34th Street and Girard Avenue
Philadelphia, Pennsylvania   19104

World Wildlife Fund (Canada)
90 Eglinton Avenue East, Suite 504
Toronto, Ontario M4P 2Z7

THINGS TO DO

These projects are designed to help you have fun with what you've learned about small cats. You can do them alone, in small groups, or as a class project.

1. Spend a day at the zoo. Find the wild cats exhibit. Can you identify any of them?

2. Look at a world globe or map and identify the natural habitat of each species of small cats.

3. The next time you see a house cat, notice its eyes and the shape of its pupils.

4. Have some fun listing all the "famous" cats you can remember in literature or entertainment (for example, The Cat in the Hat, Garfield, Felix the Cat, Sylvester, etc.).

5. Visit a museum and see if you can find a display of cats that aren't often seen in captivity.

INDEX